I Want to [Play Tennis]

by Ann Swanson Bartek

For my parents, Loran and Janet, who introduced me
to the lifetime sport of tennis when I was a little girl.

Foreword

In attempting to grow the sport of tennis, our greatest resource is our children.

During the boom of the late 1970s, tennis flourished because families played the game
together, which launched programs for all age groups and playing levels.

Getting families to return to the courts is unquestionably the way to increase participation in
tennis. The best way to do this is to follow the examples set by Little League Baseball, soccer
and other youth sports. Tennis will grow through activities that target children between the
ages of three and ten, and their parents and other family members will naturally become
active participants in such programs.

As the father of two children in this age group, I was inspired to work on the development
of USPTA Little Tennis™, the nation's premier tennis program for young players. Since the
introduction of Little Tennis™, thousands of children have taken up the sport. What's even
more interesting is the program's ability to rekindle parents and other adults' interest in the
game, thereby creating something that can be enjoyed and shared by the whole family.

If there's one thing that's even more certain to bring families together, it's the bedtime ritual
of having parents read to their children. Few youngsters will willingly go to sleep without a
bedtime story. Ann Bartek's **I Want to Play Tennis** will entertain children while it plants
a seed of interest in a lifelong sport we all love.

I'm happy that Ann is a USPTA member, and I look proudly upon her accomplishments on
behalf of all teaching professionals and parents.

Tim Heckler, CEO
United States Professional Tennis Association, Inc.

I want to play tennis.

When I grow up,
I want to play tennis
like Steffi or Pete
. . . or my Mom.

Oh, yeah, my name is Ali,
and this is my brother Drew.
He wants to play tennis too.

So Mom enrolled me
and my brother
in a special class
that was like no other.

I was kind of scared
the first day of class.
Mom said,
"That's okay. The feeling will pass."

The teacher said,
with a smiling face,
"Make sure you stay in
your very own space."

And wouldn't you know it?
My brother Drew
got bonked on the head
by Tami Sue.

I said,
"It's not your fault, Tami Sue, it's not."
I told my brother,
"Better stay in your spot!"

My teacher taught us how to hit a *forehand.*
She said, "Pointer finger out, swing low to high,
and lift your racket way up in the sky."

Then came the *volley.*
My teacher told me,
"Run to the net, give a high five,
and hit with a punch to stay alive."

I raced to the net and gave my best swing . . .

Uh-oh, I missed.
Did I look like a ding-a-ling?

But my teacher said,
"Ali, that's all right. You gave a good try.
Now, hit with a punch
and keep your racket high."

I peeked through the fence,
and there stood my Dad.
I hit a great shot.
Wow, was I glad!

"All right," said the teacher,
"it's time for *backhands*.
Turn to one side
and swing with both hands."

"Okay, class, we are ready to *serve.*
Toss the ball high, reach to the sky,
follow through now
and watch your ball fly."

"Forehands, volleys,
backhands, and serves.
Now, it's time to learn *sportsmanship*,
which everyone deserves."

"Win or lose,
having fun is the aim.
Be sure to shake hands
after the game."

"You will find
by being a really good sport,
you'll have more friends
on and off the court."

I like to play tennis.
This game sure is fun!
"Watch out Mom,
someday I'll be number one!"

The End

Tennis Glossary

Backhand: a tennis stroke in which you reach across your body to hit the ball; can be hit with one hand or two hands; same motion as the forehand.

Class: a group of children who are taught tennis by a certified tennis professional.

Forehand: a tennis stroke, usually hit with one hand, swinging low to high.

Serve: a tennis stroke that has a motion similar to throwing a ball; this stroke begins play.

Sportsmanship: an act of being fair; being a good loser as well as being a good winner.

Tennis: a fun game played with a racket, a ball and friends.

Volley: a tennis stroke in which you hit the ball before it bounces, using a punching or blocking motion; made near the net.

For more information on how to get started in tennis,
contact your local certified tennis professional or:

Tennis Industry Association   or   United States Professional Tennis Association, Inc.
6355 Westheimer, Suite 301   One USPTA Centre
Houston, TX 77057   3535 Briarpark Drive
(713) 781-7352   Houston, TX 77042-5235
                                                (713) 97-USPTA (978-7782)